P9-ARB-570

PAINTING WITH OILS

Art-in-Practice Series

Project Director: Edward A. Hamilton
Photographer: Burk Uzzle

OTHER BOOKS
Painting with Watercolor by Mario Cooper
Painting the Nude by Glenn Hamm

painting with oils
warren brandt

Art-in-Practice Series General Editor: Jerry G. Bowles

VNR VAN NOSTRAND REINHOLD COMPANY
NEW YORK   CINCINNATI   TORONTO   LONDON   MELBOURNE

Van Nostrand Reinhold Company Regional Offices:
New York Cincinnati Chicago Millbrae Dallas
Van Nostrand Reinhold Company Foreign Offices:
London Toronto Melbourne

Copyright © 1971 by Litton Educational Publishing, Inc.
Library of Congress Catalog Card Number 71-149250

Published by Van Nostrand Reinhold Company
450 West 33rd Street, New York, N.Y. 10001

Published simultaneously in Canada by
Van Nostrand Reinhold Company Ltd.

16 15 14 13 12 11 10 9 8 7 6 5 4 3 2 1

CONTENTS

The ART-IN-PRACTICE SERIES introduces a staff-oriented approach to the design and editing of art instruction books. For each book in the Series, a well-known creative artist and acknowledged experts in the fields of book design, professional writing, and photography have combined their talents in order to render the most effective and stimulating learning experience possible through the printed page. Integrating print and pictures for a unified graphic design; capturing in writing the distinctive atmosphere surrounding the artist, as well as his techniques and instruction; visually documenting the artist at work and his step-by-step processes through dynamic photographs—these are the important visual-editorial concepts of the ART-IN-PRACTICE SERIES.

What will future art historians say of Warren Brandt?

They will say, surely, that he was a man who loved painting, who loved the concept of what an artist is; that he was a great colorist; that in an age of super-hyperbole he was a man who remained true to his own instincts.

They will say that he was an artist who continued to grow throughout his career, a man who believed change to be an inevitable and personal evolvement; that he painted pictures that made people happy.

They will say these things because they are all true today.

But, for those who have been lucky enough to know Warren Brandt, to share his enthusiasm for life and art, there is much more. The man and the artist are inseperable: Brandt is Southern grace wed to an intuitive sense of order. He is committed to the pursuit of his vision of the truth and to excellence in the grandest sense.

Brandt's roots are in the paintings of the turn-of-the-century French masters, particularly Matisse and Bonnard. Yet, he hasn't been content to merely repeat history; he has contemporized the intimist's genre to produce extraordinary pictures that are fresh and new.

The range of his palette seems limitless. Kenneth Sawyer, writing in *Art International,* said, "No one in the United States today, I think, has Brandt's command of color." John Canaday, in *The New York Times,* said Brandt produces "paintings of great coloristic vigor, firmly engineered as compositions, but with a most agreeable final air of buoyant high spirits."

His subjects may, at first, seem slight—still lifes; relaxed figures reading, lounging, sunbathing; beautiful nudes in classical poses. In Brandt's paintings, however, the content is irrelevant. The subject of his paintings is painting.

Brandt is probably the best painter of women alive; almost all of his paintings with figures are celebrations of the female form and mystique. His admiration for women is linked, no doubt, to that almost peculiarly Southern idea that a beautiful woman is—in addition to being an individual—a precious, sensual, mysterious object, something to be admired, loved, painted, and preserved.

The facts of Warren Brandt's life are rather well known. He was born in Greensboro, North Carolina, in 1918, received a B.F.A. degree from Washington University in St. Louis (where he studied with Max Beckmann), and an M.F.A. from the University of North Carolina. Before arriving in New York in the early 1960s, he headed the art departments at four universities, including the university of Mississippi and the University of Southern Illinois. Today, he divides his time between his spacious studio and home in Water Mill, Long Island, and his Manhattan townhouse studio. He is represented in New York by A.M. Sachs Gallery.

Brandt is a gentle bear of a man who enjoys life and people and art. In the creative sense, he is a restless man who is constantly refining his craft and sharpening the range of his imagination. He is an artist who has never stopped growing in creative power and, as a result, his current paintings are his best ever.

It has taken Warren Brandt nearly two decades of painting and teaching to discover what he does best in art. What Warren Brandt does best is oil painting, traditional easel painting developed out of the French tradition but updated and personalized. He is an artist's artist and his mastery of the intimist genre is simply unexcelled.

Jerry G. Bowles
New York, 1971

1. A Philosophy of Painting

Why do artists paint?

The answer is simple—they paint because they have to. That is where the simplicity ends, however. The artist is an intense, complex, often egocentric individual who is prone to question almost everything. The good ones are dedicated, hard-working, sensitive, and aware of the beauty of things that surround them.

There is no easy way to paint. Obviously, no one book can teach you everything there is to know about the creative process. This book is about how one man—the author—thinks and feels and practices his art. It is an attempt to bring thirty years of painting experience and fifteen years of college teaching experience to bear on some philosophical and technical problems of art. I intend to tell you how I work and also quite a bit about how other people approach similar problems. From this, hopefully, you will be able to find your own way. That is the goal for which you should aim.

There are no hard-and-fast rules about painting, but there are some things I believe about the nature of painting.

I feel that through the painting of objects—still lifes and figures—you can come to understand color and form and that this experience will be useful no matter what kind of painting you eventually evolve into.

I believe that art is an extension of nature, that art is form and so are life and nature. The complex system of relationships that make up one, make up the rest. Because of this, painting is not so much a reflection of nature as it is a continuation of nature. An artist must inject his own pulse beat into his work so that it becomes completely organic. Art must carry on the life process.

To bridge the painter and the painting, there must be an urge to paint. This indefinable, germinal force lies within the artist. It is nature that activates this impulse. "Nature" is all of the universe as we know it, and reality as we feel and accept it. Nature is the source of all art. An artist is someone who can transpose and order nature into a perceivable object of aesthetic merit.

There is so much confusion in the art world at the present time that the wise artist is one who feels obligated to himself to do what he likes, can, and wants to do. Fashions and fads are becoming less important. Everyone is free to follow his own direction and this has been a healthy thing for the art community.

In my work, I have gone from a realistic to a nonobjective and back to a realistic approach. It seems to me that an artist must be open to change.

My more recent paintings have been compared by some critics to those of Milton Avery, Bonnard, Matisse, and Vuillard. Like these painters, I utilize the things and people around me as subject matter.

My paintings, although they look simply constructed, are actually highly structured—an influence, no doubt, of Max Beckmann, who was one of my teachers.

The large abstract canvases that I did in the 1950s may, at first glance, seem far removed from my recent paintings. But, look closer. From each painting an artist does, he should learn. I took certain solutions to painting problems that I had learned in the fifties and incorporated them into my new paintings. Over a period of years, an artist learns those things that are important to his work. The style of presentation may change, but the goal remains the same. The goal is the creation of a unified, exciting painting.

The artist changes, he grows, and responds to his environment (or in many cases, he actually perceives a change that is yet to come). The true artist is never satisfied and through his constant exploration of the world, his work must change.

After many years of painting, I have distilled what is important to me in life and in art—my family, lovely objects, a quiet life. These things I paint—in the most traditional of all media—but they are a unique expression of my vision of reality.

For some years now, people—mainly in New York—have been proclaiming the demise of easel painting. Oil painting in a traditional sense is dead, they say. But, of course, they are wrong. Oil painting and easel painting in general are in a very healthy state.

There is a reaction to the easy, flamboyant, attention-getting art of today and this reaction is leading younger artists back into more formal—and in my opinion—more serious areas of study. This serious approach has already begun to be the new avant garde in American painting.

This book does not supply all the answers. It is not intended to do so. It is, hopefully, a helpful guide based on one artist's experiences and represents only his personal approach to painting.

In the final analysis, every artist must find his own way, his own style, his own manner of approaching the creative process.

Max Beckmann once told me when I was his student: "Form many versions of reality in order to find yourself." In short, don't be afraid to attempt impossibilities. This advice remains as true today as when he said it over twenty years ago.

Before applying the final touches to a painting of a nude, I prepare the paint on the easel. White should always be mixed with other colors.

Facing page, *Daffodils and Forsythia,* 1970. Oil, 22″ x 18″. Collection of Mr. and Mrs. Jerome Myers, Chevy Chase, Maryland. This simple subject is made complex by the use of the patterns of the Persian rug on the table and the one in the background which form a dark shape that creates movement toward the bottom left corner. The movement is counterbalanced by another movement between the small dish, the orange, and the pitcher of flowers, and it is the tensions between them, as well as the objects within them, that create a dynamic composition.

Ellen, 1968. Oil, 36″ x 29″. Collection of Mr. Jerome Kohlberg, Jr., New York. Notice how, in this picture, horizontal and vertical planes can be played against a soft curved figure—a contrast that I use frequently. Light is contrasted with dark and the relaxed form against a highly controlled space.

Facing page, *The Paisley Bed,* 1966. Oil, 50'' x 40''. Collection of Mr. and Mrs. E. M. Black, New York. In what is an intimate but formal composition, the large curved form of the rug contrasts with the rectangular form of the bed, and patterns of light lead the eye through the picture. The floor and paisley patterns become almost abstract, but the major elements are kept unified.

Two Girls, Red Screen, 1970. Oil, 54'' x 60''. Collection of the artist. The picture, which is based on a horizontal-vertical plan of lines running parallel to the edges of the canvas, also has the figures, pillows, drapery, and dog creating a circular balance.

White Robe, 1968. Oil, 26'' x 24''. Collection of the artist.

Both of these pictures were arrived at quickly but seemed complete; so I left them as they were. The color is simple and helps carry the mood. In neither case was I attempting to paint a particular woman, but rather to convey a mood and an attitude as an excuse to employ color and form.

Model in Repose, 1968. Oil, 36″ x 40″. Collection of Mr. Harold Sonners, Beverly Hills, California.

Blue Bottle, Blue Cloth, 1970. Oil,
20'' x 26''. Courtesy Agra Gallery,
Washington, D.C. A very close-up
detail of the picture gives a feeling
for the texture and brushstrokes
of which it is composed. It is also
a good example of how dark and
light contrasts build excitement.

2. Drawing

The best way to learn to draw is to study the approaches of the great masters. Who are the masters? Well, that's a matter of personal preference. Everyone will have a different set of artists with whom he feels a kinship and who he feels have created significant work. Form an impression of the kind of drawing you want to do and when you come across an artist's work—in museums or books—that you like, study his approach as hard and as much as you can. It doesn't hurt to copy as long as you do it in the sense of study.

Although there has been a tendency to deemphasize drawing, it seems to me to be an absolute prerequisite to painting. To artists the word means organization of ideas in a linear and plastic sense.

"Plastic," in the painting sense, means giving life to something that, although stationary, has the possibility of illusion of movement. Great drawings, like the kernels of great ideas, are plastic in the sense that they allow and create movement. They not only show structure, but they also suggest how objects can bring life to space.

There is no art in simply copying something exactly as you see it in real life. A camera can perform that function much better than any painter. The artist must "interpret" what he sees and present his audience with his own special vision of the object in question.

In the beginning of my career, I was particularly attached to the drawings of first Toulouse-Lautrec, then Degas, and I made many studies and sketches from their work and tried to make paintings as much like theirs as possible. I find myself still going back to both of them all the time for basic pleasure and instruction.

Drawing from nature taught them, and can teach you, what forms look like and can create in your mind a reservoir of forms that can be used in imaginative work and even in very abstract painting. Most often, I don't use drawings directly to paint from, but rather as exercises in seeing.

An artist should always be looking, measuring, seeing, and putting things down on paper. Quick sketches in which you try to immediately catch the essence of a subject in a few meaningful lines are invaluable. They give you ideas for paintings and they help you when you paint. The good painter, because he understands planes and colors, does not have to labor his drawings when organizing a canvas. A rough outline of shapes and spaces will often do fine.

One useful exercise in drawing is to draw with charcoal

on a piece of paper, partially erase what you've drawn, and draw again on top of it from a slightly different point of view. With these overlapping lines the object will begin to build up a solid plastic shape. Keep doing this and soon you will begin to understand something about form.

In using drawing as a beginning for a painting, put down something that you see until you begin to find an idea. The process itself will often suggest directions if you simply let your mind remain uncluttered. Soon, something will suggest a certain rhythm or order—which line should be emphasized, softened, left opened, enclosed—so that an interlocking of shapes, planes, masses, spaces, and lines takes place and the picture begins to take on that plastic sense. You will soon realize that there is more than one way to begin.

The suggestion of planes, through tones, in drawing creates the feeling of solidity in the form and shows you what the shape of the form is. With only a few planes, one is able to suggest shape and mass. Sculptors' drawings show this clearly and should be studied for this purpose.

Movement in drawing can be created also by the use of darks and lights in both planes and lines. The effect of skillful use of this technique is that the eye moves from line to line, mass to mass, plane to plane. The tensions created by these in-and-out movements help give life to the space. The shapes of the in-between spaces are as important and help to create movement as much as the positive shapes. The study of abstract art and design help us to feel this totality of space.

A line that completely encircles a form usually cuts that form out of relationship with other forms. Beginners often feel that it is necessary to outline every object. Unless used as a stylistic device, this tends to separate each part from the rest. Lines should be used to show edges, as shown in the drawings on pages 20-21. The drawing should always be related to the edges of the paper. Every space, positive and negative, is important to the whole.

Different artists use drawing for different reasons. Matisse used them not as ideas for paintings, but as exercises. Picasso uses them for both ideas and exercises.

Drawing is invaluable as an indication of the structure of a painting, to point to its accents and planes and rhythms, and can be a determining factor in suggesting the direction of a painting.

I have been labeled a colorist in painting and I am, of course, guilty. But, drawing is equally important, if not more important. It is both the organization of the total space or the formal part of a painting and it shows the shape of a particular object in a painting. Regardless of style, good drawing is absolutely essential.

Page from sketchbook, 1970, Paris. Pen and ink. It's possible, as this sketch shows, to get down the feeling of a scene with just a few lines. Pen and ink is an excellent medium for this type of fast observation.

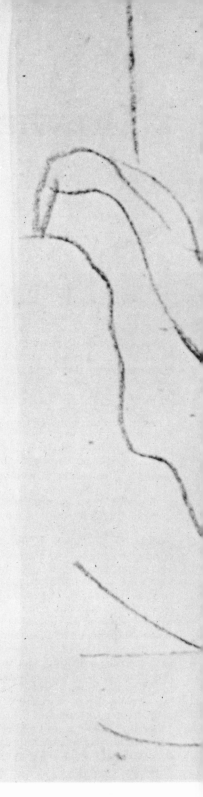

Sketch of a man by Toulouse-Lautrec. Pencil drawing. Notice how Lautrec established the essence of the character with a few strokes, delineating both the composition of the page and the form of the object.

Sketch of pigeons, 1970, Paris. The action, the grouping, and the placement on the page were all I had time to get down, but, these are the most important things in starting a drawing.

Study of a model, 1969. Sepia crayon. Again, I was attempting to quickly get down the essentials of a subject and at the same time create a rhythm using the objects that are there. You can create dynamics of space relations as much by what is left out as by what is put in.

Pencil drawing by Henri Matisse. Matisse's drawing is a beautiful example of how simple lines can convey a feeling of solidity and form. The slight shading around the shoulders helps create the feeling of volume.

Two Models. Pencil. In this figure study, I intended to indicate how the proper aspects of rhythm, line, and tone can be unified to create character, a sense of space, and the illusion of volume. The models, particularly the one in the foreground, seem solid although only simple line and shaping were used.

This charcoal sketch for a painting of two models in Oriental costumes was done mainly to indicate grouping. I often use such drawings to determine where figures should be placed and what kind of space should be left around them before moving on to the actual painting.

Sketch of lunchroom, 1970. Black conté crayon, with touches of gouache. Rijksmuseum, Amsterdam. The division in the big room between light and dark was the thing that excited me and I tried to get that in the composition. Notice the darks that move into the figure of the man on the left and the lights that move through the figure of the woman on the right.

La modèle dans l'atelier by Edouard Vuillard, 1895. Pastel and crayon, 8'' x 7''. Similar uses of dark and light and composition relate this work to the drawing at left.

25

Page from sketchbook of drawings of family, 1965, Water Mill, Long Island. Pen and ink. From this slight sketch and knowledge of the scene and people, I was able to paint a complete picture of this subject later. As you can see, concentrating your art on the things that surround you works to your advantage.

Japanese print, eighteenth century. Diagonal lines which seem to move have been used to create a sense of space.

Pencil Study of Flowers by Vuillard. In this quick sketch, notice how the dark shading adds contrast and drama. The dark spots create a circular rhythm that gives the simple subject an exciting movement.

Sketch in Amsterdam Restaurant. Ink and watercolor. Again, dark areas create a movement that carries the viewer's eye around the page.

Sketch of Men Talking, Thassos, Greece. Watercolor and pencil. Here, the circular movement created by the dark areas is balanced by the series of vertical panels. A good drawing or painting will always have balancing elements which hold together as a unit, for without them, there is no drama.

3. Organization of Pictorial Space

Form is a highly complex system of relationships involving not only structure but also rhythm and meaning and much that is simply undefinable.

In painting, the artist may start with the form that is suggested by something that he has chanced to see and from that point develop the picture through the gradual enriching of a single idea.

It is the artist's feelings about the world and his personal experiences that are the motivation and energy source of his paintings. A vase of flowers near a bowl of fruit may evoke an aesthetic excitement because of their relationship to each other in space. This relationship starts the form-making machinery.

The painter sees form in terms of contrasts; in pine trees, dark and linear, cutting sharply across a gray or blue sky; in the movement of people against environments.

In looking at an object, we are able to distinguish it because of its dark and light tonal contrasts. A simple way to look at it is this: Light is light because it is next to something that is dark, and dark is dark because it is next to something that is light.

The artist uses all the contrasts available to him in the making of a picture. We use warm against cool colors, dark against light; we use soft shapes against hard edges, smooth surfaces against rougher ones, line against volume.

If these devices are used properly, the object being painted seems to become a solid form. Contrasts help create the movement, the excitement, of a painting and help the artist to control what is happening on the surface. A painting is, after all, a flat plane, but it must seem to have volume. Contrasts help create this illusion of depth and space.

By putting a light next to a dark color and moving into a halftone and then another halftone, one can create movement both in and out and across the surface of the painting.

In my work, I strive to create a horizontal-vertical contrast primarily by moving shapes in and out and around within this grid. Unless a canvas is a perfect square, the first contrast—the shape of the painting—has already been made for the artist.

More than anything, contrasts create tensions that bring excitement to a picture. Forms push out and pull back depending upon emphasis, tone, and color. Pure symmetrical balance can be a deadly thing in painting. Great pictures are achieved when their elements are dangerously and precariously balanced.

A painting may be, at one stage of its execution, a swirling mass of chaos held together only by the fragile belief of the artist that he is on the right track. It is only the painter's feeling for balance and rhythm—which is felt rather than intellectualized—that can bring order to a painting.

A simple subject, a vase of flowers and fruit, can be as profound as any complicated abstract subject if it expresses the feelings of the painter. The beginning painter should exercise great care to avoid falling into theoretical traps. One's feelings toward an object are the only real and true guide to how an object should be painted.

As you paint, allow yourself to be open to what happens on the canvas and remain free to move outside of the objects you are painting by allowing the contrasts and movement to assume control of the design. When something happens that just spontaneously seems right and gives you an idea where to proceed, follow that impulse and move with it until you sense the need for counter-movement. If a particular movement gets too strong, look for a contrasting element that will bring the picture back into harmony.

In short, begin a painting with a limited game plan. Don't try to plan exactly every movement, every brush stroke, every shape, in advance. Things happen on the canvas for those who are flexible.

Always proceed with the idea of constructing an object that is exciting because it has balanced tensions. Start with one simple idea and keep it simple.

Let one element of the painting at a time be your focal point and then move on to something else when your intuition and experience tell you the time is right. Balance color with form, plane with line, back and forth, until a dynamic harmonious solution has been reached. There are absolutely no rules that will give you the key to achieving this balance.

Organizing space on a canvas is the most intuitive of all the elements involved in making a picture. No one can tell you how to do it in a way that will be uniquely yours. The search for an individual solution to this problem is, perhaps, the most challenging of all painting problems.

You must look for yourself; the search is a highly personal one and the manner in which you work it out will determine just what kind of an artist you really are.

The most important thing to remember is that the finished painting must be plastic—that is, a living, breathing, moving thing capable of arousing in its spectators an awareness of the artist's feelings about the world.

Azalea Plant, 1970. Oil, 36″ x 32″. Collection of the artist. There is a kind of oriental simplicity in color and motif to this picture.

Blue Still Life, 1970. Oil, 48″ x 52″.
Courtesy A.M. Sachs Gallery, New York.

Still Life on Rug, 1970. Oil, 20″ x 24″.
Collection of Mr. and Mrs. Kalman
Gitomer, Elkins Park, Pennsylvania.

Each of the three paintings show a different approach to the problem of still life painting, but they all achieve the same end—a unified whole. It's true that the objects vary from painting to painting, but also the ways of organizing them are endless, as well as the possibilities of color. It's not the choice of objects or their placement that is the essential thing; it's how you discover within the objects a rhythm, a color idea, and with these elements strike a balance that gives the painting life.

Studio, 1970. Oil, 50″ x 60″. Collection of the artist.

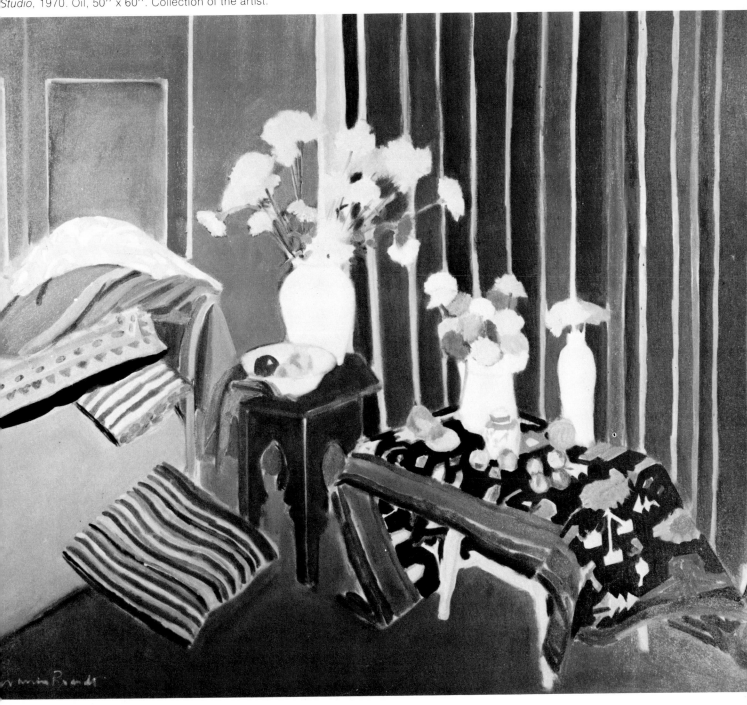

Girl with Flowered Robe, 1968. Oil, 20'' x 24''. Collection of Mrs. Robert Dowling, New York. Mood is an important aspect of the totality of painting, and in this picture, the girl's expression and surroundings all contribute to the atmosphere. Mood plays an important part in the creative process, since it is something that begins to come out of a painting as it develops and it can be strengthened and changed as the picture progresses. Mood, color, light, and space are all within the artist's province to bring to a painting and they are all results of artistic bent, hard work, and originality. In talking about space, it is easy enough to point out that one object in front of another creates depth. The picture plane acts as the first plane and everything placed on that canvas and into that plane creates depth. Also, there's a rule that warm colors come forward and cool colors recede. But I happen to believe that space is created through the completion of the painting, by the artist making the painting work, and in no other way.

36

Checkers, Water Mill, 1969. Oil, 36″ x 40″. Collection of Mr. and Mrs. Bernard Brown, Vineland, New Jersey. One of my favorite themes is to have figures enclosed in a room with a window leading outside. The inside-outside motif helps create a tension of movement back into space which is countered by the horizontal-vertical movement throughout the picture and the interior movement of the figures. The objects outdoors relate in structure to the objects inside and create a flat space, where, in actuality, they appear to be in deep space.

In a linear analysis of *Studio Corner II,* note the strong, dynamic diagonal movement.

Facing page, *Studio Corner II,* 1970. Oil, 40″ x 30″. Collection of the artist. Based more on diagonal movements rather than on a horizontal-vertical plan, the mood in this work is evoked through color, which is rich but subdued.

A form analysis shows how color, shape, and pattern were the basic inspiration for the painting. Colors were kept flat and simple, with thin second coats modifying the original colors until harmony was achieved. By placing a large area of light on the left, which juts into the dark area on the right, a large and interesting balance of areas was developed.

I took this photograph of the models in Water Mill, Long Island.

The problem of painting directly from two models in the studio has occupied me for some time. Beginning with a beautiful subject—the girls, flowers, objects—the major problem is to keep the picture both beautiful and strong by the proper use of formal relationships. Ideally, the subject loses its importance as these formal elements take over and the painting becomes the subject.

Two Models, *Oriental Costumes*, 1970. Oil, 40" x 50". Collection of the artist.

Two Models, *Oriental Rugs*, 1970. Oil, 50" x 60". Collection of the artist.

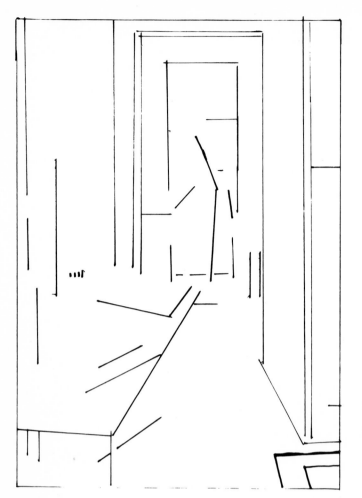

A straight-line analysis of the painting on page 43 shows that the diagonal lines seem to move back in space while the lines parallel to the edges seem to be on the picture plane level.

A curved-line analysis demonstrates that the curves throughout the painting seem to have a basic rhythm.

After the Shower III, 1967. Oil, 70″ x 50″. Collection of Dr. and Mrs. Joseph Coker, Mount Vernon, Virginia. This painting is a good example of how the problem of deep space has been solved by holding the major elements of line, color, tone, and light to the picture plane. The rhythm of the movement of line to line, color to color, tone to tone, remains on and across the surface. The integrity of the surface has been maintained and a tension has been created between what we feel is deep and what we know is flat. Hans Hoffman called this space contradiction ''push-pull,'' and it is this, more than any other factor, that brings life to a pictorial space.

4. Color

Color is the most individual and personal aspect of painting. Each person has preferences as to what he likes and dislikes. The artist with creative integrity will choose to use those colors that he prefers. To not do so almost inevitably dooms his paintings to failure.

My color preferences are rather obvious, if you look at the color photographs in this book. I like contrasts of colors. I like colors that are built up by painting one contrasting color over another. I like a certain vitality and richness and luminosity. I like color with body and in washes, if it is good color.

I do *not* like dull or sunken colors or colors that are too grayed.

I begin a painting by putting down a color that I like and then adding another color that goes with it. This can either be a complement or another color from the same family. By this method of constantly adjusting and balancing, the color gets richer and better.

Don't be self-conscious about the use of color. One should never fear washing out or painting over any color that doesn't seem right. If you return to a painting and find a color or shape that simply is incorrect, the first thing you should do is change it to bring it into harmony. You may find that by changing one color, another needs changing also. Then you have the glorious prospect of changing each color until they all sing together.

When they sing, the painting is finished. As Cézanne said, "When the color is right, the painting is finished."

There are no hard-and-fast rules of color. What should be done, how one should go about doing it—these are questions that each person must decide, depending upon what he wishes to say in painting. If a certain brashness is what is desired, then use strong tones. If quietness is the desired effect, use harmonious colors. In short, it is possible to create an exciting and beautiful picture with tones of gray and equally possible with brilliant, contrasting colors. Which you prefer is up to you.

The rules of composition apply equally to the rules of color. Excitement is brought about through contrasts, tone, harmony, and disharmony. A yellow that is surrounded by other yellows might not be seen, or it might be very exciting.

Black is the ultimate contrast and can make any color look good. From this, one can deduce that dark and light is one of the most important elements of color relationships.

Model and Yellow Table, 1965-1967. Oil, 24" x 26". Collection of Mr. Harold Sonners, Beverly Hills, California. In this painting, which took two years to complete, colors were painted, scraped off, painted over, changed again until the day the picture seemed just right. With color, it is important to know when to stop—but also, by the same token, when to continue.

Matisse said that knowing that a blue makes an orange jump, or vibrate, is a good rule. But, he said, knowing the rule means nothing. How the rule is handled in practice is the major point.

To elaborate, color contrasts are what make a painting exciting to a significant degree. A red next to a green of the right intensity, a purple next to a yellow, an orange next to a blue—these relationships are exciting. But the thing that makes them so is the personal manner in which these ideas are achieved.

In painting, white is the best additive to color to give it both body and light. A little of it should be mixed with every color.

Each painting has its own particular color problems and it is essential to approach each one with this in mind. No rules can automatically solve problems of color and composition for you. Each painting is unique.

The local color I try to keep, but I change it enough to make it fit into the total color harmony as the picture develops. It can be a red apple, but it has to be a red that harmonizes or contrasts or acts vitally in the painting. If you can make a red that does this in that particular spot, then why not make the apple red? If you can't, however, make the apple whatever color fits the need of the situation and works in the particular context.

Copying nature exactly will not give you the harmony, the totality you need. On the other hand, looking at nature should tell you all there is to know about color. See for yourself what seems to be exciting and what seems to be dull. I have found that all colors go together, can be held together, and can be made interesting by weighing their proper substance and value. Nature is not necessarily art, but a source for art.

The light, the mood, the union, the contrasts are what make it art. The red of the apple has to be worked out until it achieves its place in the total picture. It shouldn't fall out. It must exist not as an apple, but as part of a unified painting.

In short, the meaning comes not from the apple, but from the form, the color, the line, and shape and the way these elements interrelate to the whole.

A series of realistic objects unrelated to each other in terms of line, color, shape, mood, and light do not make a painting. The fact that the color of the apple is one thing or another makes little difference in the final analysis.

Remember, however, that every picture must exist as a unified whole. It has to have an overall totality. Each artist, according to his own feelings and views about painting, brings a different feeling to these objects, this space and light. But if it feels right to him, holds together for him, then it is a true work of art.

The two photographs depict my palette at the beginning of the day and the way it looks at the end of a painting session. Notice that I keep my colors in groups. The warm colors are together—beginning with dark reds and moving through yellow greens. From there, I go into the cool greens to the even cooler blues, and on into the black. There is no absolute formula for setting up a palette; it simply is up to each painter to determine where he likes his paints. It is important, however, to always keep them in the same place, so that you will develop the habit of knowing exactly where each color is and won't have to take your eye off the subject very often. The white paint in the center of the palette is put in several spots because then each spot can become the basis for a particular kind of blended color. I have built a wooden shelf on the front of my easel for holding the palette and other materials, and now I no longer need to turn away from the picture as I used to when I had the palette on a table off to the side.

At top on the facing page is a simplified color wheel showing the major colors and their complements. The diagram below represents what might well be a typical arrangement of colors on a palette. Notice that the colors are arranged in groups moving from one end of the spectrum to the other.

I mix a small amount of dammar varnish into a standard flake white while I prepare for the first day of painting, in order to help the paint dry fast and make a good working consistency for the initial laying in of colors.

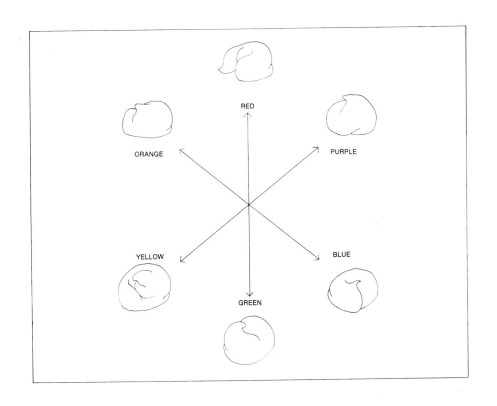

RED

ORANGE

PURPLE

YELLOW

BLUE

GREEN

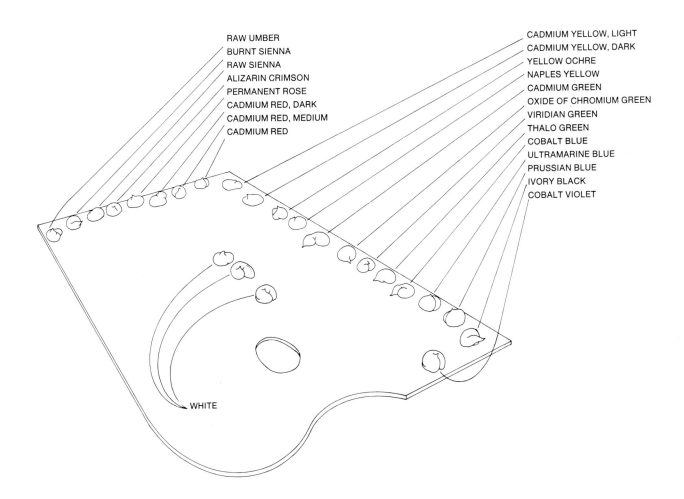

RAW UMBER
BURNT SIENNA
RAW SIENNA
ALIZARIN CRIMSON
PERMANENT ROSE
CADMIUM RED, DARK
CADMIUM RED, MEDIUM
CADMIUM RED

CADMIUM YELLOW, LIGHT
CADMIUM YELLOW, DARK
YELLOW OCHRE
NAPLES YELLOW
CADMIUM GREEN
OXIDE OF CHROMIUM GREEN
VIRIDIAN GREEN
THALO GREEN
COBALT BLUE
ULTRAMARINE BLUE
PRUSSIAN BLUE
IVORY BLACK
COBALT VIOLET

WHITE

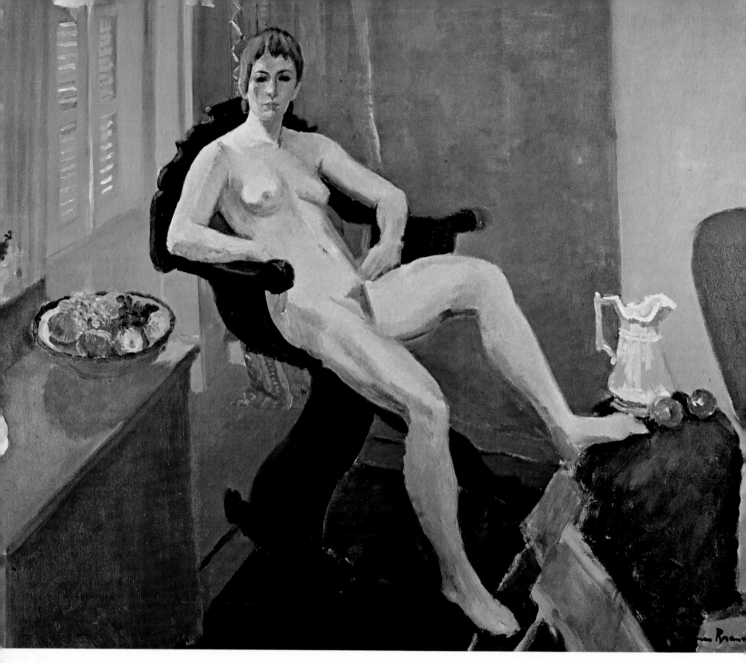

Kilina, 1971. Oil, 30″ x 36″. Courtesy A. M. Sachs Gallery, New York. Although it has complex color, the painting reads simply. The color of the model's red hair, which is extremely appealing, is repeated in elements of the environment and the dark chair acts as a contrast to her light skin.

Still Life with Zinnias, 1968. Oil, 30″ x 36″. Collection of Dr. and Mrs. Abraham Cohen, Washington, D.C. Almost a study in curves, the picture is nevertheless held together by the dark horizontal and vertical shapes in the background. There is also a tight color relationship between the background and the objects in the setup.

Pink Roses, 1970. Oil, 30″ x 34″. Courtesy David Barnett Gallery, Milwaukee, Wisconsin. This is an illustration of how very simple objects can make a beautiful painting. Pink is a color that can be most effective when used sparingly.

5. How to Begin a Painting

To try to express how a painting is conceived is to belie the uniqueness of its creation. It is just as impossible to explain exactly a color relationship as it is to explain the nuances of a human relationship. The artist can report *how* but not *why*. But, of course, every painting must have a beginning. It is the first stroke that breaks up the old order and is the genesis of a new one.

When beginning, try to get things down as quickly as possible, develop the idea, and keep it moving. Sometimes you may get stuck immediately and nothing happens. Rather than force an image, it is better to put it aside and begin with another canvas.

In sketching in an outline on the canvas, make each object as general as possible. Keep it in line and keep it simple. Divide the space into its major areas; think of the canvas as a space to be filled.

If you are drawing a still life, the divisions might be the top of a table, the corner of a table, the wall behind, or other simple points of reference. Then indicate as simply as possible the main objects on the table (or whatever you happen to be looking at). Put them down with a light line so they can easily be changed. If you are working with paint on canvas, keep the paint thin, use one color, and keep a rag handy for wiping out in case you need to change something. Keep adjusting the objects until they feel correct and properly related. Relationships at this point are the most important element. After the objects are properly placed, then you can search for a more exact definition of edges.

There are many ways to perceive a painting before it is started—from sketches, from life, from setting up certain objects in the studio, or in the field.

I have used all these methods. Sometimes I start directly with color, sometimes with a black line drawing, simply laying out the shapes in more or less the way they should be on the canvas; sometimes with pastel on canvas in one or two colors; sometimes with paint thinned with turpentine; sometimes with fairly thick paint; sometimes on a colored ground; sometimes on white canvas.

If I see two beautiful colors next to each other—say, a beautiful yellow apple against a purple rug—this may be the trigger that will make me start off immediately with a yellow and a purple next to each other and this will be the key throughout the painting. Every other color then becomes related to these two exciting colors.

Another time, the visual stimulus might be the rhythm of certain flowers as they move into space and as they relate

A good model will serve as a visual stimulus.

to other forms in the picture. Sometimes the rhythm might be the most important element and the prospect of organizing the painting from the standpoint of rhythm might set me off.

This is one way to begin. Make a drawing with a brush dipped in turpentine and blue paint. Draw loosely, suggesting where you want the major forms to be. Using a rag dipped in turpentine, change the forms from one place to another until you find a grouping that feels right. If your key objects are too large, too small, too much to the right or too much to the left, move them around. It would be a good practice to go through this beginning exercise many times before actually starting to add color.

When you feel the drawing is good, choose one color or color combination that you like best and put down that color or those two colors on the object. Proceed from there and work in small patches which indicate planes; these patches build forms while creating movement at the same time. Put down the rest of the colors, making sure that they relate to the two colors that you began with. Proceed patch by patch and put color over the entire surface. It is more important, remember, to keep the colors relating to your key colors than to paint the colors the objects actually are.

Remember that, in the early stages, you need to find in what you are looking at some elements of contrast, harmony, and order that make what you are painting interesting to you. Try to get this feeling into the picture as fast as possible because it will tell you where to go with the rest of the picture. A painting needs a key idea—not a story or literary quality—but something abstract such as a movement of shapes, contrast of colors, or a dominant image which can bring to the painting the life that it needs.

Every day, the painter goes into his studio ready to paint. His mood, the weather, the thoughts that are going through his mind, the painting left unfinished from yesterday—all these play a role in the work he will do today. Maybe, he will want to work on a new painting, but his attention is caught by one on which he has been working for a long time. So he leaves the new to consider the old. In looking, he sees that what seemed yesterday to be almost right is, today, not good at all. He begins to work. The first strokes or color changes may be deliberate, done in the faith that they will solve the problem, but the slightest change of one part means that the whole will have to be changed. The artist finds himself working more quickly and any single part becomes less important than the whole. No shape is worth saving if it does not fit the emotion. The paints seem to mix themselves and the color that is needed suggests itself. It is at this point that one becomes an artist.

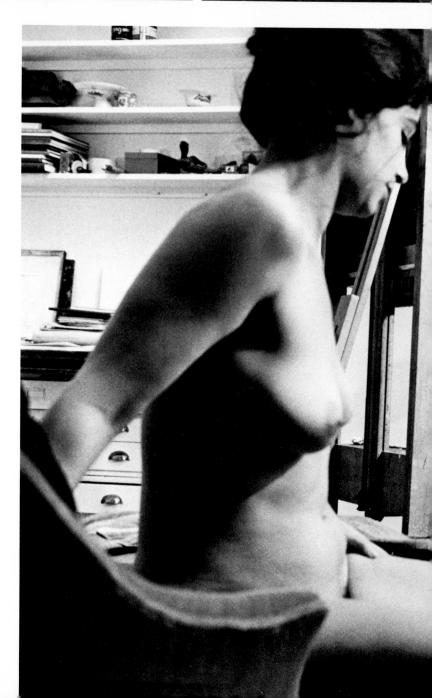

In figure painting, it is essential that you get a model you enjoy looking at and that you establish a rapport with her. I work in a studio situation, surrounding the model with romantic, beautiful, and exotic objects. This gives you an atmosphere in which to begin.

The model assumes a natural, simple pose.

The first lines on the canvas, which are most important, should be kept simple, as you adjust the figure to the space, wash it out and put it back until an idea of movement and design begins to develop and the main areas are established.

With a rag dipped in turpentine I can change lines and color.

I put colors on lightly in washes to suggest local color and movement.

I indicate the planes to show the shape of the forms.

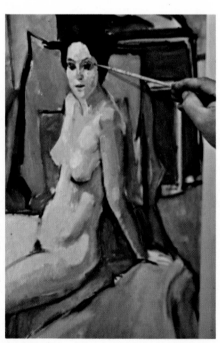

As the painting progresses, a constant adjusting or balancing of line to color, color to color, light to dark takes place, and parts are changed or removed as the idea grows. Making a painting is a growing process and what you end up with may be quite unlike the idea you had in the beginning. Allow your mind to flow with the things that happen on the canvas.

6. Finishing the Painting

The second day is usually a tough one in the life of a painter. Coming to the painting with a fresh eye, it's quite possible to see things that require drastic change. If the painting is still wet—and it probably will be, using oil—this is not as hard as it may seem. You can wipe off some of the paint with turpentine on a rag or scrape it with a palette knife or single-edged razor blade. While doing this is a good time to take a hard look at the picture and see if you can improve what has been done so far.

If the painting is dry, changes can still be made by painting over areas that need to be changed. Before doing this, however, it is a good idea to scrape the area with a palette knife or razor edge to roughen the surface slightly so the new paint will adhere.

Wet or dry, colors can be changed—and probably should be—to enrich and strengthen the total effect of the color. Sometimes this calls for a complementary color over the color that's already there—say a purple painted into a yellow—or sometimes just a deepening or lightening of the original color is needed.

If the color needs changing completely, it is a good idea to scumble, which is to put a layer of transparent white over the area, and then repaint new color back into the scumble. The color should still be visible through the white and you can allow the underneath color to come through by using a rag to thin it in some places. Using this technique, it is possible to get a great variety of colors by using only a few. The combination of the underneath color coming through the white veil and the color on top creates a heightened effect of depth and luminosity and interest.

A glaze on the other hand darkens a color. It is a color made thin by mixing it with oil or oil and varnish. It is wiped or rubbed over areas in a painting and brings about a rich deepening of a color. It can be the same color, say a dark alizarin red over a lighter red, or a different color, say an alizarin over a light green—which, because it is transparent, seems optically to become a gray.

Glazes over areas can—like a scumble—bring unity, but one has to be careful that they don't darken the picture too much. The way to avoid glazing the picture too darkly is to add a touch of white or some other more opaque color, such as Naples yellow or yellow ochre, to the glaze color.

Just a little opaque color will give a glaze body and keep it from being too shiny. Scumbling and glazing are extremely important in creating visual depth in painting. By put-

ting a slightly more opaque color over the glaze in places and working glaze and opaque, glaze and opaque, the resulting in-and-out tensions will create a flow instead of just a glassy overall surface.

A glaze, like a scumble, can be put on with a rag, wiped off in spots so underneath color can show through, left on, or painted into. Be careful, however, that the color you paint into a glaze is not too dry or it will show up as a dull spot in the total surface of the painting.

This method of painting is a slow working buildup in which layer after layer is put on until the painting is finished. The other traditional way of painting is *alla prima,* in which the painting is worked on directly, wet into wet.

Sometimes, a painting can be completed in only a few sessions. Other times, it might take weeks or even years. I keep many pictures in progress at the same time. Some I might do a few things to each day and others I might work on two or three hours or two or three days at a time.

In working this way, the picture takes on the characteristics of emotion, rhythm, color, and form that the artist has felt. When finished, the picture has an existence of its own. It is neither the artist nor a reflection of him; it is a separate form that exists within and outside of time.

If the artist establishes within the picture an essentially lifelike relationship and if the picture is a complete entity, then the spectator can enter it.

It is important to be able to deny your intellectual concepts of what would be right in order to use your intuition as a painter. Sometimes the thing that intellectually appears to be wrong winds up being the strong element that unifies and pulls the painting together.

We're not talking about making a *beautiful* painting, but a thing that exists with a reality that is different from other realities. Sometimes a painting that does not seem finished or is somehow disturbing won't let you work on it further. At this stage, it's probably finished.

Feeling is all important. Often, you feel something is wrong in a picture, so you change it. This changes the emphasis and makes it necessary to change something else to go with the first change. Perhaps you'll wind up repainting the entire picture around that one change. But nothing really matters except that you wind up with a total.

In my work, I try not to change the subject, only my approach to the subject. My problem is, most often, the adjustment of colors and shapes until they fit each other, not the subject.

In order to reach the point of completion in a picture, you must depend largely upon intuition. But, you must also have all the training and knowledge of your medium that you can acquire. This, and only this, allows you to pull it off.

I always look at a painting I'm working on upside down, because it makes it easier to see the formal ideas and the color relationships, rather than the obvious subject.

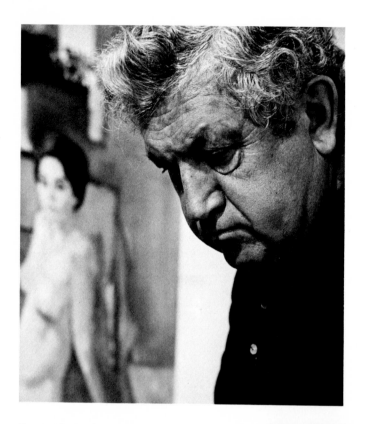

A good artist is seldom, if ever, totally satisfied with his work. The process of change and experimentation is a constant one as, trying to find the right way, he moves into new forms and back to old ones.

By standing or by sitting on a high stool I am able to get a deeper perspective than if I were on the same level as the model, and being on a higher floor plane helps me to create the feeling of studio space that I want in the final painting.

Always welcome the process of change and, since there is no one right answer, continue to search.

Facing page, *Model with Purple Screen,* 1971. Oil, 36″ x 30″. Collection of Mr. David Barnett, Milwaukee, Wisconsin. There are really no definable means for a painter to know when a picture is completed except by intuition and experience. The great thing about painting is that there are an infinite number of ways a subject can be treated and many of them would be equally successful. If the painting is unified, has elements of excitement, and feels right to you, then it is complete.

7. Still Life

The setup is an important aspect of still life. Find a few objects that you like and feel are related and put them together on a table. Choose objects with a variety of shapes and colors, some harmonious, some contrasting. Find within this group certain formal elements such as parallel lines, continuing lines, dark and light patterns, contrasting tones, movement of shapes and objects, oppositional forces, and color contrasts. All of these things make the objects relate to each other and create the tension of the picture.

If the canvas is horizontal in shape, arrange the still life horizontally. Do the opposite if the canvas is vertical. This is the general idea, to think of the horizontal or vertical axis of the canvas, but not to arrange specific objects. A flower arrangement that's too prearranged generally doesn't make for a good still life because it's too ordered in the beginning to allow the artist's imagination to move.

After the setup, begin to draw broadly in simple shapes and lines in one color thinned with turpentine. Select the one object that seems to you to be most important, or simply the largest, put it down and then arrange the rest of the shapes in relation to that major thing. Change the positions as many times as necessary until you feel that all the elements are working together. Begin to establish the various major planes and then, as you move along, the smaller planes. Try to determine the main axis of each object (the line that runs through the middle in its major direction) and establish that in relation to the other objects. This helps you see the relationship of each object, helps you draw, and helps you feel the force of the direction of that object.

In painting, one of the major elements of organization is directional movement. This is true in still life as in all other kinds of painting. Each object tends to move in the direction of its central axis. This movement then becomes the force in moving the eye of the viewer in a horizontal, vertical, or diagonal direction. The play of these forces against each other is one of the key things in creating dynamic movement. The eye can be led through this by curving lines.

The same kind of movement of the eye of the spectator can also be created by objects that are alike in either size or color or by joining two or three such objects of similar colors together.

Highlights or light spots can also create movement. Repetition of lines, parallel lines and parallel objects can all create movement through the similarity as well as the

Still Life with Carnations, 1970. Oil, 60″ x 50″. Collection of the artist. In this typical still life, the straight horizontal and vertical lines are balanced by the roundness of the various objects.

sense of rhythm that they help to create. This movement and rhythm can be done in many ways. A small object related to a large object or a small line repeated by a large line, opposed by another line, are examples of how the rhythm is established, much the way that a loud and a soft sound are balanced in music.

After you've made the initial drawing with thin blue or black paint, use the rag to rub in an indication of planes to help establish the shape. At this stage, keep the rag handy in order to make changes, to rub out, or move the color.

Work tentatively at this stage, putting down colors, feeling if they're right, establishing shapes.

Don't work on one object at a time until that object is finished. Try to move around from object to object and see the painting whole. Like a gigantic jigsaw puzzle, it gradually will all come together.

The next stage is putting on color in a slightly heavier state. Use a fairly large brush like a ½- or ¾-inch flat bristle brush. Color should be mixed with white paint that has been made lean by some dammar varnish and a little turpentine. To facilitate drying and to add body to the colors, a touch of this should be added to each color as it is put on.

Keep moving over the canvas. If you add red in one place, look and see where else you might be able to use red to create movement between the two points. Begin to establish color and tonal contrasts. For example, next to an object that is orange an indication of blue on the outside of the orange helps the orange become more visibly active.

Remember that you are drawing and painting at the same time and that it is necessary to put a dark outside a light edge to see the light edge; in color, the same principle holds true by making the tone darker and complementary—in other words, a deeper tone of a complementary color.

At this point, begin to exaggerate certain colors. Make them darker, more intense, lighter, more subtle, in order to heighten the compositional effects.

Line should be considered a moving device in the painting and not something that cuts off one object from the rest. In painting an object, it is important that tones and colors from outside move into the object at light points and at dark points. In this way, forms begin to interlock with each other and hold their place in the harmony of the total picture without being seemingly too distinct and by themselves.

As you work, certain shapes of light or color begin to relate to each other to form bigger shapes and these bigger shapes become a dominant movement. This acts as an organizing factor; these major shapes of light and dark or major divisions of color hold the picture together.

Facing page, *Still Life with Poppies,* 1970. Oil, 24″ x 18″. Collection of Mr. Thomas Tanty, Milwaukee, Wisconsin. You can use colors that are rich and sensuous in a still life and create the same color pleasure level that can be attained with a figure painting.

Imari Vase with Iris, 1971. Oil, 52″ x 48″. Collection of Mrs. Grace Borgenicht Brandt. In this painting, notice how the major divisions of color—the tablecloth, the backgrounds—refer back to the colors in the objects in the setup. It is this almost-intiuitive sense of color relationships that holds the painting together and makes the illusion of a myriad array of colors work.

Above. When putting together a setup, try not to overarrange the objects. They should give off an air of casualness, as if they had just been discovered that way by the artist and were then captured in paint.

Facing page. Here I begin to draw broadly in one color thinned with turpentine, and I keep the shapes and lines simple. After I've selected the object I consider major, I adjust all the other shapes in relation to it. This process may be very fast or it may take a great deal of adjustment.

Think of the horizontal or vertical axis of the canvas and not of specific objects.

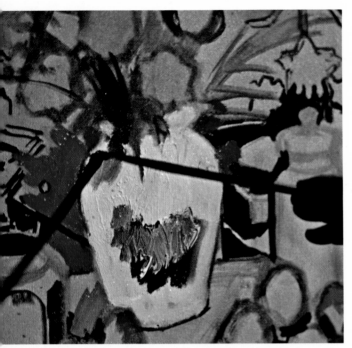

Put down the first color notation in rather heavy paint.

Continue the movement through indication of planes in slightly darker tones. The planes move across the major axis of the shape to help turn it.

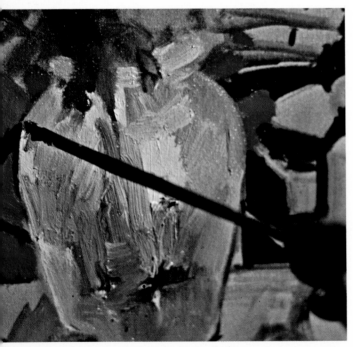

Planes of color move in and out of this major form, creating a sense of solidity as well as a rhythmic balancing of the total picture.

Introduce contrasting colors into other areas of the painting. While they may be heavy at first, they can be scraped later with a palette knife if the color needs to be changed.

It is worth repeating that the painting should be conceived of as a total and that each color tone or plane should help the movement and harmony. If you have put down the spots of color and feel that everything you could say in the painting has been said, then you should be prepared to leave it at that point.

76

Stand back and study the work from time to time, turning the picture upside down to help you see it with a fresh eye. If you look at it through a reducing glass, it will also help you see it differently. Seeing it in a mirror shows the picture to you in reverse and causes any areas that seem to fall out to reveal themselves more easily.

Facing page, *Blue-Striped Tablecloth,* detail, 1970. Oil, 30″ x 26½″. Collection of Dr. and Mrs. Benjamin Narodick, Milwaukee, Wisconsin. In this detail—from an early stage of the execution—you see the design and color begin to take shape. Note also how stylized my objects become, although in the final version there is the illusion of realism.

Blue-Striped Tablecloth, 1971. Oil, 30″ x 26½″. Collection of Dr. and Mrs. Benjamin Narodick, Milwaukee, Wisconsin. The completed version of the painting, shown from a more normal viewing distance, still conveys a sense of looseness in the forms and shapes, but enough detail has been added since the previous stage to make the painting function not as an abstract but as a representational picture.

8. Figure Painting

Figure painting, it seems to me, is the most challenging and interesting problem that a painter can attempt.

I like to get one or two models that I feel sympathetic with and enjoy looking at—not necessarily beautiful, but with some of the qualities that match my feeling about what makes beautiful form. It is absolutely essential that you work with a model that you enjoy painting.

Generally, I work in a studio situation, surrounding the model with various objects that are romantic, beautiful, and exotic. This gives the whole atmosphere of what I am looking at a creative jumping-off point and makes me want to paint what I see.

The problems you face in figure painting are essentially the same as those in other styles, but they are complicated by the fact that if you paint the model too realistically or too beautifully or with too much individuality, the work becomes mere portraiture and loses that element of universality that marks true art. Therefore, you have to find the *essence* of the model rather than the details of her features to create this universality.

Once again, the principles of picture construction hold in that you must create movement, interesting shapes, beautiful color, all in proper and constructive balance. To do this with a model is difficult because you are likely to become too involved with such problems as how an arm is contructed or how a leg is shaped or what the face looks like and forget to add each part to the totality of the picture. In painting, each part must be as important as each other part. This does not necessarily mean that each part has the same emphasis, but it is as important to the total structure.

Remember the rules of contrast. Without a subdued part, the emphasized part will not be as brilliant. Without darks, the light will not be as important. The figure must flow and fit and stay in its proper place in the space you create around it. For these reasons, it is not important in figure painting that the figure in the painting be realistic or exact, but that it is a well-integrated part of the total picture.

As you're working, regardless of whether it's figure painting or still life, it's good to paint away from the model some of the time. Instead of concentrating on what you see, this allows you to bring out ideas you have from within yourself.

Put a girl in the corner of the room as your model and without seeing her as a formal element in your work, she is just a girl in the corner of the room. The great pleasure in painting is transforming this sensuous thing that you are

In the beginning stages of a sketch for a painting, I work quickly with charcoal.

looking at into an even more sensuous thing to be enjoyed. The reality becomes the truth. After all, art is made of dreams. The male artist who paints women is looking for the eternal dream.

Paint and color in themselves are sensual elements. Making them flow, join together, be rich, transparent, opaque, putting cool colors next to hot colors, creating moods through color edges and shapes, curving soft billowing colors and shapes against rigid hard edges—through all this, the feeling of sensuality that comes from looking at beautiful women can be conveyed.

Somehow a painting of a model has to go beyond the moment into timelessness. The painting should give off the feeling or sense of mystery. The ideal to strive for is a woman who is beautiful and solid, but not of the *moment*. She is universal.

The model becomes timeless when the artist has made her an integral part of the painting. She is no longer a woman, but an element that fits with every other element that makes that strange and mysterious thing called a work of art. She is no more important to the total picture than the sofa she is sitting on or the pillow she is next to. Yet, they are not more important than the figure, either. They are all there because they have to be there. In short, the ideal is to make the model an abstract, an essential, flowing part of the total picture.

Her color is used as a complement to all the other colors used, just as they complement the colors used in the model. The curves of her body may be used as a contrast to straight lines used elsewhere in the painting. She's not a woman, she's an abstraction. On the other hand, she is Woman. What I really try to retain about the model is the mystery of woman, not the substance of a particular woman.

Mystery in painting is a powerful force. Personally, I don't want to tell a whole story. I want a general mood that springs from the joyous and proper combination of all the elements.

The woman plays a role, just as an apple plays a role in a still life. She is the subject of the picture but, more importantly, she is also a part of the bigger subject—the picture itself. While she is the starting point for the painting, painting is really the subject of painting.

There are no set rules for the formation of a figure painting. The compositional guidelines used in still life and other methods still apply. But, if the painting is well-composed and tight and has a feeling of order in a structural sense—if it is moving and exciting and beautifully painted, the possibilities of approaching the subject are varied and inexhaustible.

I choose costumes, drapery, and furnishing for studio setups that are exotic, sensual, and colorful, so that they will animate my imagination.

85

Often, models will naturally fall into a pose you like. Most, however, will require some direction as to exactly what you have in mind.

Sketch quickly and simply at first, getting down the feeling of the scene.

Two Models in Oriental Costumes, 1971. Charcoal. At this point, I felt the drawing was complete. Although the lines are still simple and there is little shading, a mood is captured.

Red and Black, 1967. Oil, 20″ x 18″. Collection of Mr. and Mrs. Turner Catledge, New Orleans, Louisiana. With the face and figure deliberately unspecific, the forms of the picture verge on the abstract. The contrasts between the black background and the white figure add a sense of drama.

Two Models in Harem Costumes, 1970. Oil, 50″ x 60″.
Collection of the artist. Again, faces are kept nonspecific
in many of my figure paintings, since I am interested not
in achieving a likeness, but in capturing the quintessential
qualities of womanhood.

Facing page, *Seated Nude,* 1970. Oil, 30″ x 24″. Collection of Mr. and Mrs. Park Nichols, Palm Beach, Florida. This is another example of how you can create the feel of realism without getting too involved in the problem of "likeness."

At right, *Red Studio with Model,* 1967-1970. Oil, 12″ x 15″. Collection of Mr. M.G. Herbach, Jenkintown, Pennsylvania.

Below, *Nude with Orange Pillows,* 1970. Oil, 12″ x 14″. Collection of Mrs. Lois Kushner, Bala-Cynwyd, Pennsylvania.

In both pictures, the models are at ease, shown in relaxed, natural, straightforward poses. I don't go in for painting athletic or exhibitionistic poses, since I prefer to let the grace of the figure speak for itself.

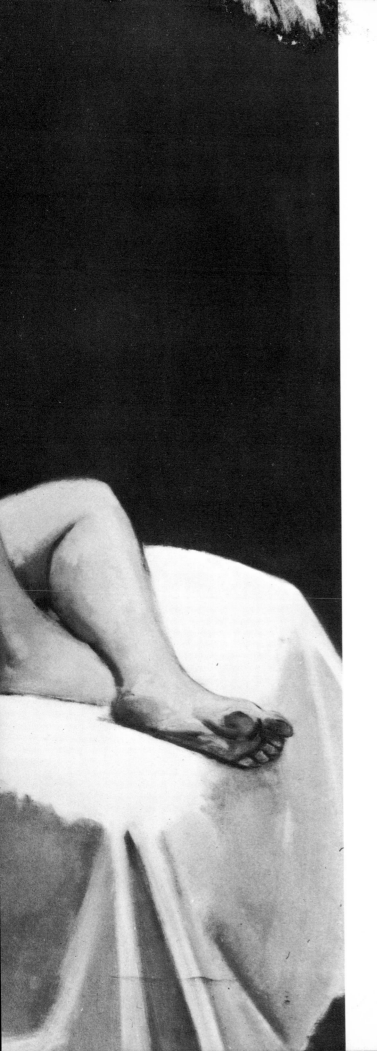

Reclining Model, 1970. Oil, 36″ x 40″. Collection of the artist.
In this study in balances, the curve of the model's body is
repeated in the curve of the drapery, while the vertical lines
of the legs are echoed in the background.

Model and Red Pillows, 1971. Oil, 26″ x 30″. Courtesy
A. M. Sachs Gallery, New York.

The two paintings demonstrate the use of similar elements—a lone figure in practically the same environment
—and how they can create two very different paintings that
nevertheless both reflect the artist's personal style.

Seated Girl by Window, 1970. Oil, 36″ x 30″. Collection
of the artist.

There is a great sense of peace and awareness that comes from being surrounded by art. I find myself always going back to the work of the masters for pleasure and instruction.

9. Portraiture

Modigliani once painted a portrait of Jean Cocteau and when asked about it, Cocteau said, "It doesn't look like me, it looks like Modigliani, and that's better."

Cocteau had perfectly understood the painter's crisis in portraiture.

The main thing to bear in mind when painting portraits is that *your* painting has to be more important than a mere likeness. Like a good figure painting, it has to be a work of art first and a resemblance second. Almost all great artists have done portraits, but they were done in the artists' styles and are therefore works of art.

As a young painter, I did many portraits but gradually gave them up because I wanted my work to be more personal and not to have to meet the demands of the sitter.

Sir Joshua Reynolds summed it up beautifully when he said the definition of a portrait is a painting with something wrong with the mouth.

In beginning a portrait, decisions have to be made as to what you want the person to wear, whether it fits in with your idea of color, whether you want the sitter to be in your studio, or whether you would prefer the subject in his own surroundings.

It is wise to begin with a series of drawings in order to get to know the sitter better and to find the arrangement, and to study the characteristics of the sitter. The drawings are like a preliminary study and are an invaluable aid in determining what you are going to do. I don't personally approve of working from photographs, although in portraiture sometimes one must.

When drawing or painting the sitter, choose a position so that the model is on the same eye level as you. If the model is sitting, then perhaps you should sit to paint. Any other way would be distorted and difficult to work out unless you choose to do it that way for some stylistic reason of your own.

Most of the portraits I do for pleasure are done from sketches that I make of my family and friends in normal, quiet activities such as reading, sitting, or listening to music.

When drawing, sometimes it is good to exaggerate the characteristics of the sitter in almost a caricaturish way in order to capture the essence, not the likeness, of the model.

Once the drawing is complete and you feel that you understand the subject, begin to paint, using the same methods you would use for any other approach. Remember

methods you would use for any other approach. Remember that the better your drawing is, the more likely your painting is to be successful.

The individual problems such as how to paint hair and how to paint skin or other details have to be thought of in the same way that one thinks when painting an apple or a flower. I like to think of everything in terms of volume and line, but another artist might like to make it flat or simple colors. I suggest that you begin by thinking in terms of volumes and planes, thinking of the face and the body as solid round shapes which are made up of small, flat color planes—planes which move into one another, some lighter, some darker, giving the essence of roundness and carrying the color throughout the painting. This was Cézanne's method and it was the basis for all modern art.

If the prospect of painting in color bothers you, do the portrait in black and white, using a little red or blue mixed with your white to either warm up or cool the composition. After this is dry, paint on top with the colors you want to use. Ingres used this method to divorce the drawing from the later coloring.

As when working with still life or the figure, you have the choice of either using the buildup or *alla prima* method. Perhaps, this would be a good time to say a little more about these technical approaches.

The buildup method, derived from Titian, involves working fairly dry in the beginning, letting that stage dry, scumbling and glazing as you proceed, painting into the scumbles and glazes each day but letting each layer dry and then proceeding in a slow building manner until the painting is finished. In general, this is the way I work. Colors can be made rich and full and harmonious through this method and it allows for a more reasoned approach.

The other classical way of painting is known as the *alla prima* technique, and we have talked about it a little before. *Alla prima* means that the work has been completed in one stage, always painting wet paint into wet paint until the completion. Slower-drying oils help to keep the paint from drying overnight. An *alla prima* painting can be worked on for days continuously so long as the paint has not really dried.

You can combine these two techniques by using the buildup technique for the underpainting and then finishing the picture using the *alla prima* method.

One last thought on portraiture. If you paint a portrait, you should do so because you like the sitter or because it brings you pleasure. If you allow yourself to be commissioned to do a portrait, you open up the possibility that the sitter will be telling you how it should be done. Since few people know what they actually look like, this can have disastrous effects.

Moroccan Costume, 1970. Oil, 16" x 14". Collection of Mr. and Mrs. Bernard Brown, Vineland, New Jersey. Although this is not really a portrait, it does convey a mood and feeling that emanate from the sitter.

Self-portrait in pen and ink.

At right, a pen sketch of a couple on the bus in Paris, 1970. Simple lines create a mood.

Below, a pen-and-ink sketch done on wrapping paper on the bus, in New York City.

Pencil drawing, Amsterdam.

Pencil study of the head of a model.

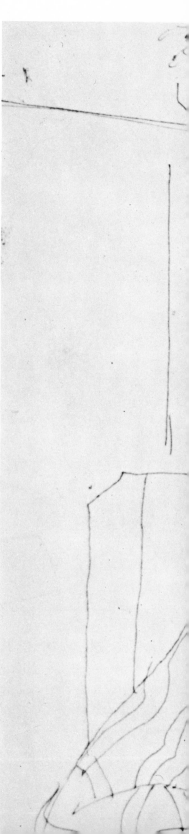

These are all studies of people done quickly to capture a mood or ambiance. The greatest challenge in drawing a portrait is to capture the feeling of a subject with a minimum of lines and shapes. It is this heightened simplicity that most informs the work of Matisse, who was certainly one of the greatest draftsmen who ever picked up a pencil.

Sketch of Lois reading.

Girl in Green Robe, 1968. Oil, 16″ x 12″. Collection of the artist.

Even though these paintings are not portraits, I think that by stressing the overall mood and ambiance given off by a person, rather than a specific likeness, you do more justice to the sitter and to your artistic impulse. That is why I prefer this kind of objective instead of the strict interpretation of painting a portrait.

Model in White Robe, 1969. Oil, 24″ x 20″. Collection of the artist.

Pencil portrait of Grace Borgenicht Brandt, 1960.

Lois, 1967-1968. Oil, 36" x 34". Collection of the artist.

As opposed to the paintings on the two previous pages, the sketch and painting of members of my family bear more specific resemblance to the sitters.

The model is photographed in pose for the portrait on the opposite page. In the first blocking-in, I attempt to get a feeling for the organization of the space. Then, by the end of the first day, the major tones and colors have been indicated.

Suzanne, 1971. Oil, 30″ x 26″. Collection of Mr. and Mrs.
Jerry Bowles, New York. The final version of the portrait shows
how much can be revealed about a particular person without
getting too involved with exact physical detail.

10. Style

What is style and how do you get it? That's a question that has troubled artists for hundreds of years.

The artist does not intellectually plan to do one thing or another; he does not arrive at any particular style through a conscious thought process. Your basic instincts, attitudes, and feelings should be the instigator of a personal style.

When the artist approaches his painting intellectually, putting ideas ahead of emotion, trusting intellect over intuition, his paintings lose their validity. Art comes from the creative use of work.

Ideas that arrive in a spontaneous manner can lead to bigger ideas or to the further use of similar ideas in other paintings. Ideas should be generated out of paintings, not put into paintings.

Approach pictures openly and allow them to affect your consciousness in such a way as to create an awareness within you that dictates the form the paintings are to take. Through this approach, you begin to see nature with your own sense of form, and personal style then becomes possible.

In my work, I have reached the point where I want to set up a still life that might have been used two hundred years ago and paint it freshly, using my background and training to give it life. Looking backward this way can sometimes mean looking forward. While I might be using the same form and subjects used by Chardin, Cézanne, and Matisse, it is as impossible for me to paint like Matisse as for Matisse to paint like Cézanne or Cézanne like Poussin. We are all different people and we all lived in a different age. The colors and the forms, the rhythms cannot help be of the time in which they are painted. With the world seeming to turn more toward technology and mass thought, I find myself, more and more, doing just what I feel like doing.

As I have said before, the great springboard to creativity and to style is nature. From nature—the raw mechanics of the life process in operation—comes the desire to make something. Out of nature, I draw my inspiration. I see a landscape, spaces between trees, women on a subway, something that strikes me as new and fresh and begging to be put down. I am able to do this, because I have found a "style," forged from observation and hard work. It is a thing that came with time.

A work of art is a measure of space, and it is form. As organized relationships between shaped areas in space, it makes its own order: form. This order demands a tangible structure. Style is variable, rather than absolute; it defines

As I look at the pictures I have painted over the years, I see what has happened in terms of change, and I get ideas for new changes.

the quality of growth and change in the artist's work.

The term style has two almost opposite meanings: in the generic sense, the word "style" implies superior quality, universality, unchangeable validity. In the other sense, style is a development, and it is with this meaning and its emphasis on the important system of relationships in evolution that I concern myself.

Style can't be sought by the artist. It must come of itself. The artist aims for it only in that he works always toward wholeness.

The style of the painter may evolve in the vigor and sureness of a technique, arriving out of a harmonious relationship between the tool and the hand, matter and form.

The hand is an extension of the mind; the brush is an extension of the hand; the touch of the brush shown by its paint traces the mind's activity.

The total unity which is present when the painting is finished eludes the painter whose personal style has not evolved. Style evolves when the balance struck between technique and feeling becomes uniquely his own. What the artist sees and hears while this is happening may come into the picture, but he is also aware of the recurrence of certain forms and colors which have become assimilated with his whole being. In the emergence of overall form there are present these insistent personal forms. They show themselves consistently through an artist's work. In the work of some artists—the good ones—these forms signify him more readily than his signature.

The artist acknowledges the importance of the intuitive. He believes that painting, through form, is an extension of life. He welcomes change because he knows life is in constant motion. He believes that paintings are to be looked at and enjoyed rather than talked about.

The rules that I think are most important in painting are the rules of the medium. The artist is limited only by the degree to which he can manipulate paint. Anybody can create anything he wants to so long as it is well done and works.

Style is a matter of taste. The artist brings to every canvas he works on his own private feelings about the world. He organizes and arranges those feelings on the canvas. Through painting, he conveys his feelings to other people.

A painter's style is his voice, his own unique way of communicating with the world.

A painting is the artist's expression of the way he feels about life. If art is considered a continuation of nature, then the artist is a link between nature and art. The content and form of his pictures—the way he puts them down—are really an extension of the life process. That's what art is really about.

An artist should always be looking, measuring, seeing, and putting things down on paper. Quick sketches in which you try to immediately catch the essence of a subject in a few meaningful lines are invaluable.

Two studies of a model singing by Edgar Degas. Charcoal and chalk.

Nude by Milton Avery. Ink.

Above, sketch by Eugène Delacroix for the Apollo Gallery, the Louvre, Paris. Red chalk.

At left, *Seated Nude* by Henri Matisse. Charcoal.

Below, *Woman* by Willem DeKooning. Ink.

It is the artist's feelings about the world and his personal experiences that are the motivation and energy source of his paintings.

Lila Reading, 1967. Oil, 42'' x 36''.
Courtesy Agra Gallery, Washington, D.C.

Still Life with Mums, 1970. Oil, 12'' x 14''. Collection of Mrs. Grace Borgenicht Brandt.

Begin your painting with a limited game plan. Don't try to plot exactly every movement, every brush stroke, every shape in advance. Things happen on the canvas for those who are flexible.

Facing page, *The Bath,* 1969. Oil, 24″ x 14″. Collection of Mr. and Mrs. William Allis, Milwaukee, Wisconsin.

Below, *Lois on Red Sofa,* 1967. Oil, 28″ x 36″. Collection of the artist.

My feeling about space and light is that they are the most ambiguous things in a painting. The space of the picture is the creation of the artist who makes the picture, and each painter makes his own space.

Facing page, *Pale Nude,* 1967. Oil, 36″ x 30″. Collection of the artist.

Below, *Daffodils and Oriental rug,* 1970. Oil, 34″ x 24″. Collection of Mrs. Samuel Reiver, Merion, Pennsylvania.

Still Life with Canton Pot, 1971. Oil, 26″ x 30″. Courtesy
A. M. Sachs Gallery, New York.

The rules I think are important in painting are the rules of the medium. The artist is limited only by the degree to which he can manipulate and exploit paint.

Wicker Chair into Dining Room, 1967. Oil, 61½″ x 69¼″.
Collection of Mr. and Mrs. Walter Scheuer, New York.

Ideas that arrive in a spontaneous manner can lead to bigger ideas or to the further use of similar ideas in other paintings. Ideas should be generated out of paintings, not put into paintings.

Isabella and Lois, 1968. Oil, 50″ x 60″. Collection of Mrs. Alan H. Polkes, New York.

The Fan, 1966. Oil, 40″ x 38″. Collection of Mrs. Alan H. Polkes, New York.

A painting is the artist's expression of the way he feels about life. If art is considered a continuation of nature, then the artist is a link between nature and art.

11. Materials and Media

It has been said that you can paint with anything that sticks. Paint is oil added to pigments of various colors. The paint is either drier or wetter depending upon the amount of oil added to the pigment.

Painting should be done in a fairly liquid state—not so wet that it slides and not so dry that it is powdery, but in a state that is somewhere between liquid and solid. This is one reason oil paint is such a marvelous medium. Through the use of this contrast of wetness and dryness, forms can be built up that have the solidity and movement and color of life.

In the beginning of a picture, paint should be fairly dry. Therefore, the paint can be made leaner by thinning it with turpentine or by adding a small amount of varnish which will facilitate drying.

There is a rule in oil painting that fat should go over lean; paints with more oil are fatter than paints with varnish. The successive stages of a painting should contain slightly more and more oil, but never to the point where oil causes the paint to slide off the surface.

Most tube colors as purchased today are loaded with oil and white is no exception. For that reason I like to put out overnight the quantity of white that I think I might be using for the next few days on a blotter or a piece of absorbent paper. This takes out some of the excess oil. Then when I start to work the next day, I mix with the palette knife a small amount of dammar varnish and a few drops of turpentine. This makes a fine white with which to begin the painting. This faster-drying paint enables one to start the underpainting rapidly and with great ease.

With this heavy white, you can build up opaque areas which will dry quickly and which are easily thinned, if you need thinner white, with a touch of oil or turpentine.

With a drier first-day painting, it is possible the next day to add a touch of oil to your white and to continue to work on a half-dry painting. The next day add a touch more oil and continue the same way. This way, the slower-drying paints are constantly being put onto faster-drying paints. Cracking occurs in a painting when an opposite approach is used—that is, when fast-drying paints are put on top of slow-drying paints.

In the latter stages of a painting, thicker oils (sun-thickened oil and stand oil) can replace regular linseed oil if you want a slow drying time and a fused look to your work.

Do not ever use acrylic paints on top of oil. This will ruin the painting.

The materials you need for oil paintings are:

paints	oil
brushes	palette
canvas	rags
turpentine	varnish

Paints can be bought in many different qualities. For the beginner, the inexpensive qualities are adequate, but more expensive paints, especially the European-made ones, have much more tinting power than the less expensive student kind. In the long run, you can get better quality and better value from the best paints. Because a good-quality paint can be extended more, it is not really that much more expensive.

A typical list of colors would include:

Naples yellow	cobalt blue
cadmium yellow (medium)	cerulean blue
cadmium orange	chromium oxide green
cadmium red (light)	burnt sienna
cadmium red (deep)	raw sienna
alizarin crimson	yellow ochre (light)
French ultramarine blue	English red (light)
rose madder	raw umber
zinc or titanium white	mars black

If you're beginning to paint, use a simple palette of white, black, red, yellow, blue, orange, green, and violet and through experience you will learn how to mix the various colors from these. Gradually, through experimentation, pick out other colors that you like and add them to your palette.

A palette can be anything that holds paint—wood, paper, or a piece of glass. They are also sold commercially, of course. Large gallon cans of a good grade of turpentine are recommended instead of the smaller bottles.

Canvas can be canvas boards, lengths of cotton or linen canvas, presized or unsized. It is a good idea to learn to size your own canvas. Not only is it less expensive, but it also teaches you more about painting. You find out what goes into the canvas, what kind of surface you like to paint on, and you find out whether the canvas absorbs paint, projects it, or holds it on the surface.

In order to be able to improvise and to do what you want to do with painting, you must know craft thoroughly. Although craft is not the most important element in painting, it is essential to have a good knowledge of materials and technique.

The technique is the manipulation of the medium through which the artist expresses his feelings. It is mastered through feeling, which may evolve as style. Technique itself is relatively unimportant, except that through working a system is developed which better facilitates clear expression. Whatever the choice of medium, the artist should use the technique which limits his expression least.

In this detail, which reads abstractly, note the feeling of the buildup of paint produced by an impasto technique.

127

The more involved you get in painting, the more space you seem to need for all the equipment and materials. My studio in town is much smaller than this one in Water Mill, Long Island, but it also serves quite well.

129

These are some of the objects and materials I use in my paintings.

The studio, and the two models I am arranging, display some of my favored draperies and costumes.

In a photographic still life, you see more objects that I like to use in still-life setups.

This area of my work table holds some of the materials I use for oil painting.

Another section of the table shows some additional typical materials.

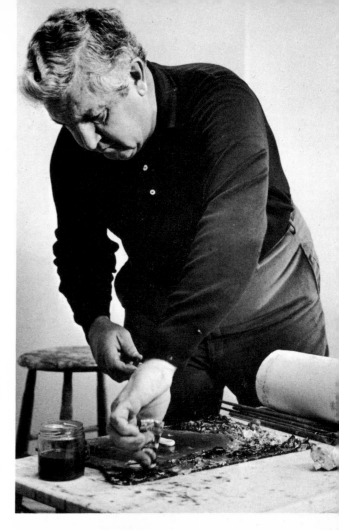

A photograph of some of the tubes of oil paints I use shows the many different brands and types that are available.

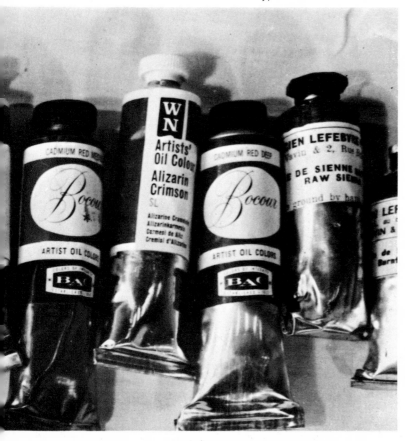

Picture Credits

The photographs of Warren Brandt on pp. 6, 8, 46-47, 48, 56-57, 58, 59, 60-61, 62, 63, 64, 66, 67, 74, 75, 76, 77, 78-79, 82, 84-85, 86, 122, 128-129, 130-131, 133, 139, and 140-141 were taken by Burk Uzzle.

The photographs of the paintings on pp. 11, 12, 88, 114, 121, 124, and of the drawing by Matisse on p. 113 were taken by Walter Rosenblum.

The photographs of the drawings on pp. 18, 20, 21, 24-25, 26-27, 86-87, 100, 101, 102, 103, 112, and 133 were taken by Dave Sagarin.

INDEX

Page numbers in italics indicate illustrations.